In The Mix: Discover The Secrets to Becoming a Successful DJ

Tommy Swindali

Copyright Notice

Disclaimer

Can I Ask You a Quick Favor?

If you like this book, I would greatly appreciate if you could leave an honest review

Reviews are very important to us authors, and it only takes a minute to post.

Download Audio

This book is also available now as an audiobook.
Head over to www.audible.com or
Download on the Audible application

Other Books by Tommy Swindali

Music Production: Everything You Need To Know About Producing Music and Songwriting

Everything You Need To Know About Making Music In One Place! Grab your chance to own this comprehensive guide by Tommy Swindali. Covering everything you need to know about music production, as well as songwriting. Find Out More

Music Production: How to Produce Music, The Easy to Read Guide for Music Producers Introduction

You are about to discover proven steps and strategies from music producers on how to produce music, even if you have zero experience in recording and audio engineering. You will be able to learn everything you need to know in order to make your first single sound just the way you want it. Find Out More

Songwriting: Apply Proven Methods, Ideas and Exercises to Kickstart or Upgrade Your Songwriting

Have you ever listened to a song and thought "wow, if only I could write a song like that"? Well, you can now learn all the secrets on how to write beautiful music with this guide to songwriting! Find Out More

In This Book You Will Discover

If you have ever dreamed of being a DJ with people dancing to your music and all whilst having the time of your life then this book will show you how. From the bedroom to the hottest clubs, events and mainstage festivals.

Whether you're a seasoned pro looking to enhance your current skills or a new aspiring DJ looking to get started. Whatever your level of experience, the wisdom in this book is explosive and it is an absolute must to skyrocketing your success as a DJ.

This easy to understand guide will enable you to master the essentials of DJing. Including, gear, music, techniques, business, and the industry as a whole. You'll learn how to research and purchase the best DJ equipment, on your budget. Where to find music, how to smoothly mix music and create solid playlists to rock any dance floor. Plus you will learn how to get paid gigs at parties, clubs, events and so much more!

Anybody can be a DJ and if you've ever wanted a single book that gives you all the secrets to a successful career as a DJ, **then this is that book....**

Contents

Introduction

A lot of people have the misconception that DJing is really hard to get into but it's actually really simple. All you need is the passion and you can start out with something as simple as a smartphone, or a DJ controller. anybody can be a DJ as long as they work hard and are motivated to achieve their goals

In essence, DJing is taking music that already exists and changing it in a way that is pleasing for a crowd. What's great about it is that you can combine different genres and songs into one idea. DJing creates this, sort of, combined culture that really unites many fans. There is so much you can do as a DJ from mixing in the bedroom to stirring up a storm on the main stage.

Nowadays, there are so many different ways to DJ. What could originally only be done on turntables, by early pioneers such as Grandmaster Flash and Carl Cox, can now be done with many more pieces of equipment. There are many amazing programs now, such as Traktor Pro, Serato and Rekordbox and even applications for tablets and touchscreens. If you prefer the old school ways you can still use turntables or even CDJs, controllers and extra hardware. There are so many different combinations. All of these really do the same thing, and that's to mix songs.

When your staring out, take the time to study DJs and find the music that inspires you. Whether it's listening to podcasts, watching live sets, or just really looking them up online. Observe and take in what it means to be a great DJ. Hone your skills with regular practice and you will soon be able to play at any club.

Festivals and club culture have created massive DJ stars and turned it into a popular past time. The current climate for is highly competitive and you will need a strategy to stand out. Because besides DJing, there are many more tasks to do. For example DJs need to promote themselves, network and maybe eventually produce music to get more gigs. Whether you are a beginner or more. experienced the contents of this book will help you.

Beginner's Guide To DJ Equipment Setups

The absolute easiest way to get started DJing is with your smartphone. There are an absolute slew of DJing apps and my favorite is Algorithms DJ. It's pretty much a fully fledged DJing solution in your pocket and is really easy to use. It features a full mixer with some effects that aren't even available on hardware and there are individual deck controls. With its Spotify integration you don't need to download music on your phone. Actually you can just download it off the cloud. If you want something more hands on then the next level is the DJ controller.

DJ Controller

If you're thinking about a DJ system for home it doesn't really make sense to have the nightclub equivalent. Unless you're making an awful lot of money from your DJing or money's no object. DJ controllers offer an affordable solution. Essentially the controller is two to four CDJ's combined with a mixer in one piece of equipment. In most you can also input microphones, headphones and output to speakers.

The controller is going to connect to your laptop or your tablet and will also be running a DJ software. You can link these up with Traktor or Serato software which will hold your library of music and allow playback on virtual decks that you control with controller. Let's take a look at the five best DJ controllers.

Newmark NVII

A dual CDJ, four channel controller. This allows you to have up to four decks playing simultaneously. Aside from looking great and offering full color screens the NBI offers an ultra fast response of operation and seamlessly beat matching to make it a strong choice.

Reloop Terminal Mix Eight Reloop

A four deck performance controller, great for mixing lots of songs. The controller was developed to work specifically with Serato DJ software and it responds well to the requirements of professional club DJ's. Offers creative effects manipulation and unique mixing possibilities.

Kontrol S4 MK2

A dual CDJ, four channel controller allowing up to four decks playing simultaneously. A great choice for DJ's who want professional features, ease of use and portability. Combines a high quality mixer with professional grade, built in sound card and an intuitive interface that works with Traktor Pro 2 software.

Pioneer DDJ SB

The best two channel option on the market. Responsive performance pads and large jog wheels make it easy to mix and mash up live music. Offers low latency jog wheels for great scratch response and accuracy. High-pass filters combined on the cross fader offer both volume and base filters with just one hand. Great for smooth mixes.

Professional's Guide To DJ Equipment Setups

The industry standard for DJ's in a nightclub is currently two to four, CDJ's and a DJ mixer which will go out to the main soundsystem. The DJ will have their own monitor feed to listen to and of course headphones to listen to the song that is not playing. Pioneer currently dominate the professional DJ equipment market. Denon are making a strong efforts but Pioneer remain king.

CDJ

The Pioneer CDJ 2000 Nexus and Nexus 2 are currently the club standard for CDJ's and will likely stay that way for the next five years.

Let's take a look at the CDJ Nexus 2. On the left side, there is a flashing USB input which shows you if the CDJ is currently in use. Upto four CDJ's can be linked together and played off of one USB. This makes it easy for the next DJ coming in to use their USB without disturbing you.

To start, first the USB stick goes in and you select a source. Select link if the USB is in the adjacent CDJ. You can select the source you are using on the buttons to the left. Which are Rekordbox, link, USB, sd, disc. Sd slot is below the USB and disc is at the bottom of the unit. Once loaded you can browse through the folders by turning the dial to the appropriate folder. When you find the song you want to play, simply press down and it is loaded to go. You can organize music to your preferences with Rekordbox software before you use your USB and then export the settings. When you finish playing there is a

USB stop switch. Make sure you hold this down and wait for it to be OK to remove.

Below the USB input is a bank of hot cues. Hot cues are great if you want to seamlessly skip forward or backwards without stopping the play. They are color-coded as well backlit. There are upto eight hot cues available in two banks. Bank two can be be found by clicking the bank buttons at the bottom. You can add and delete hot cues on the player using the controls there or alternatively before you mix using Rekordbox software.

Below the hot cues is a paddle switch to move the play direction forwards, reverse or slip rev, which is cool for quick cuts. At the bottom left you have track search and search buttons for skipping or searching through tracks. Then you have the cue and play/pause buttons. The cue button will always default to where it was last set. When you pressed it will stop there. On the right is the cue loop to shift the memory cues which are associated with the cue button. Add memory or delete is for making or deleting memory cues.

The large digital panel screen allows you to browse through playlists, select songs and organize them by your preferences. This could be by bpm, alphabet or key for example. The track filter button helps you to find tracks that are either related in key, a similar BPM or a similar rating of energy level. For example you could set it for everything in a related key plus or minus a certain bpm. This is a feature that you must setup first with Rekordbox software. If you want to search for songs there is a touch screen QWERTY keyboard. Then there is a tag list which is where you can tag tracks and dump them into a playlist whilst you're playing. This helps to remind yourself that you want to play them a bit later. The touchpad allows you to jump around the track and skip wherever you want to. If you hold down menu this is the utility where all of the settings are for various different system preferences.

When you select a track you will see the waveform which you can zoom in on and also edit it's grid settings. If a song is off the grid adjust it here to ensure your mixes stay locked in. At the top of the screen is a phase meter which is a visual reference for how the songs you are mixing match up on the grid. There are two options, one shows the beats in blocks and another shows parallel waveforms with transients. Using this reference you can see if the songs you are mixing are out of phase.

In the middle of the player is a large jog wheel for controlling the song, speed and direction. The response rate can be adjusted using the jog adjustment dial on the right. Above the jog wheel you can set up loops. There is a button here which is a for an instant eight bar loop. Press it once and it puts you straight into loop mode. If you press it whilst it's looping it will cut the loop down by a half each time. This is really cool for making build ups. There is also a loop mode next to that where you can set the start and end points of a manual loop.

On the right side of the CDJ you have disc eject for CDs. Below that is vinyl speed adjust for break and release. This determines what happens when pressing stop and start. If you have it set short it will be normal but longer settings will create a slow pitched down effect similar to how old school turntables behave. Next you have a mode for Vinyl or CD, this depends on your preferences. Vinyl is better if you want to use the jog wheel more for scratching and dropping in hip hop style. Whilst CD mode is better for continuous mixing such as with house or techno.

Next you have the Master and Sync buttons which can be used to lock your mixes together. When active, one CDJ acts as the master for tempo. This would be the CDJ that is currently playing through the speakers. The other CDJ you would be cueing up would be clicked to be in sync with the master. This will lock it to the tempo of the master and make your mixes really tight and on point. However if you have not set your songs properly onto the grid then it might not lock in properly. Always trust your ears first.

Finally we have the tempo fader to speed up or slow down playback. Use this to match bpm with the song you are mixing into. If you need more variation in speed you can increase its depth with the +-6 to - wide button. If you activate the Master tempo button then the pitch won't be affected by it. However if you want some cool effects, turn it off and use a wide tempo to create a really speeded up or super slowed down sound. The tempo reset button on the right will bring the speed back to default zero.

DJM900 Nexus

The DJM900 Nexus is an industry standard mixer that will probably be around for the next five years. It is easy to understand and very reliable.

On the top left side are two inputs for laptops. If your DJing with a laptop it allows you to easily plug in here without having to worry about a soundcard or audio interface. Below this are two microphone controls with gain, high and low eq potentiometers.

Having these is great if you work with an mc because you can both have instant control at your fingertips.

The mixer features four identical channels each with gain, three band eq, color knob, cue button and x fader controls. The x fader is the most commonly used for transitions. You can assign how slow or fast it acts by using the switch on the right side of the mixer. Quick fades are great for hip hop mixing whilst slower ones work well with house or techno. If you really like to cut in and out quickly you can use the crossfader located at the bottom of the mixer. Each channel can be assigned to be A or B or Thru. Typically you would assign them to be Thru so that they are on their standard numerical assignment. If you want to use the crossfader assign them to the A or B side of the crossfader.

There are six different sound color fx which are available by using the sound color knob assigned to each of the four channels. These include, space, dub echo, gate/comp, noise, crush and filter. Add these to your transitions by sweeping them in and out to create really cool transitions. Below the sound color fx are the headphone controls. You can mix the source with the cue channel and control volume for headphones. If you want to listen to a channel just press its cue button.

On the right side of the mixer is the master gain, left and right balance, mono/stereo switch and booth monitor gain. This is used to directly control the volume of the booth monitor. In a club or festival setup there will often be a delay between the live feed and the monitor. Make sure you can hear the monitor clearly but without damaging your ears. Below the monitor control are the intensity curve settings for the eq, x faders and cross fader. Set these depending on your mixing style.

On the far right of the mixer is the beat effects section. You can assign effects including, delay, echo, ping pong, spiral, spiral, reverb, trans, filter, flanger, phaser, pitch, slip roll, roll, vinyl brake, helix to each of the channels, microphone, or master mix. Below you can adjust the timing so that effects are occurring quicker or slower. You could for example have a quick scattered delay or a long echo. Or you could have a very sudden trans effect where it seems like the music suddenly stops like on a record deck. Or you could make it longer as if it is being switched off. Then you have the intensity knob for the effects and also an on/off button for them. This is great if you want to suddenly turn on an effect such as a quick LFO filter. Or a dramatic flange over a transition. On newer versions of the mixer there are buttons to cut the low, mid and high frequencies of effects. I recommend leaving the low cut so that you don't get too much interference of low frequencies.

Laptop DJ

Some DJ's prefer working with a laptop when mixing. The advantage to this is you can hold a lot more music and generally access it a lot more quickly and easily. It is debatable that sound quality degrades when using a laptop since the sound has been processed more. It is also important to note that using a laptop may distance you from the crowd a bit more since you would be looking at a screen most of the time. When mixing with a USB your more visual and engaged with the crowd. However if you decide to work with a laptop then the best option is to use Serato. This is a DJ software allowing you to manage and play your music library with CDJ's and a DJ mixer or a controller. Normally this can be set up by using an audio interface such as a Rane D/A Box that will connect your computer straight to the

CDJ and DJ mixer. On some DJ mixers you can plug your laptop straight in.

USB

Nowadays the majority of DJ's are playing from USB. It's possible to also use SD cards with newer CDJ's but for the majority USB is more popular in addition to being quicker and handling larger sizes for a more affordable price.

To make sure you get the best performance for your money you need to know what specifications actually matter. Storage capacity is something that needs to be decided by the individual but 32 gig is a good start. Next you want to pay specific attention to read speed and write speed. The USB 2.0 specification is 60 megabytes per second and the USB 3.0 is 640 megabytes per second. Keep in mind though that these are just theoretical and each drive is going to have its own speed that is probably a whole lot slower. Speed can help the players feel more snappy when it comes to browsing and searching for tracks and is hugely important if you don't want to spend hours waiting for your files to transfer from your software. Therefore USB 3 is the best to go with. Kingston, The Corsair Survivor range and GTX models are all great brands/models. If you find a USB that you like, buy a couple more because if stuff gets lost or broken you need to be able to keep the party going. In addition, make sure you keep your USB in its own bag or compartment to keep it protected.

Where Do DJs Get Their Music?

Where you find music depends on what you need it for. For example if you are playing a wedding, you will get music from a different place than if your playing at a club.

Many DJ's these days rip music from YouTube. **I would not recommend this.** If you're getting songs off YouTube what you're doing is you're getting it from the music videos. Sometimes in music videos, the music will stop or there might be live action sound effects or dialogue on the top. In addition music logo's might be played on the top such as the infamous Hardwell On Air logo. If you rip music straight from YouTube you will get those sound effects in the song. This is going to make you look stupid if you play it out, believe me I have seen it. The other reason is the quality is low. Quality wise you should use at least MP3 320 kbps, WAV or AAC.

The first place to find music is iTunes. If you have a song in mind and you want it quickly then you can get a high quality download there. Generally iTunes is best for pop music. If you are looking for more specific genres then Beatport is great. There are so many genres on there and you can tune into to the tastes of each genre with charts by DJ's and charts of sales. Beatport gives you additional information like the beats per minute (bpm) of the song and what key it is in. It is really easy to use and you can sign up for a free account.

The next source I recommend is DJ pools. Now if you're not familiar with the concept of the DJ pool, it's a place where DJs can get access to new music. Back in the vinyl days when record companies would plan a new release they would first press a limited amount of copies on vinyl. They would then distribute those copies among the DJ's so they could start playing it in the clubs, the radio or on mixtapes to promote it. Nowadays DJ pools have moved online and you can become a member. Most of them do require a monthly fee but you get unlimited access to a lot of music for around $20 per month. DJ pools also make special edits of songs or improve on them. DJ city is my favorite.

I also recommend you subscribe to a bunch of YouTube channels whose music you like so that whenever they have new releases you can be notified. www.souncloud.com is good too, you can find some cool, edits and unreleased things there. Just search around. Then also www.hypeddit.com is great for downloading mashup packs. If your a commercial DJ keep an eye on the trends through Billboard charts and also Shazam is cool if you hear a song you like, then it can identify it.

How to Understand Genres

Afro House
118 to 124 bpm
beat driven 4/4 music with lots of strong percussion samples and latin vocals.
popular in south africa

Prominent Artists Include
Black Coffee, Black Motion, Darque, Bucie, Da Capo, Sir LSG, Tumelo, Lilac Jeans, Jullian Gomes, Derrick Flair, DJ Afrozilla.

Big Room
128 - 132 bpm
4/4 dance floor music with big synths and big bass kicks. Popular in most large commercial clubs and festivals

Prominent Artists Include
Hardwell, Madig, Basshackers, MAKJ, Wolfpack, KSHMR, Nervo, R3hab, Dimitri Vegas and Like Mike, Martin Garrix

Breaks
120 - 130 bpm
4/4 Sample driven music with heavy live breakbeats and big baselines. Popular in USA and UK, underground clubs.

Prominent Artists Include
Plump DJs, Freestylers, Justin Martin, Stanton Warriors

Dance
122- 128 bpm
4/4 commercial sound with catchy vocal hooks or melodies over tight drums and a strong kick.

Prominent Artists Include
Tiesto, Calvin Harris, Alok, Martin Solvet, Madison Mars, Mike Cervello, Vintage Culture, Brohug

Deep House
120 - 124 bpm

4/4 simple sounds and longer transitions with lots of ambience and light textures. Popular at bars, rooftops and in the UK.

Prominent Artists Include
Audiojack, Kassian, Musumeci, Donatello, Kaz James, Matthias Meyer, Stereocalypse

Drum and Bass
172-175 bpm

High energy music with rolling drums and big basslines. Some songs are more atmospheric but most aimed at the dance floor. popular in the UK.

Prominent Artists Include
Andy C, Chase and Status, Sub Focus, TC, Rene Lavice, Loadstar, Cyantific, Mampi Swift,

Dubstep
140 - 155 bpm

Screechy sounds, huge drops, big bass and hard drums. Often features samples and catchy hooks. Popular in The USA and at festivals.

Prominent Artists Include
Zombie, Datsic, Skrillex, Virtual Riot, Wooli, Herobust, Tynan,

Electro House
126 - 128 bpm

Big beats, hard sounds, synth leads and basslines. Often very technical and high energy with lots of samples and short sounds. Popular in clubs.

Prominent Artists Include
Joyride, Curbi, Dyro, Brohug, Bingo players, Krunk, Uberjackd, Chocolate Puma,

Electronica/Downtempo
100 - 124 bpm

Electronic/synthetic minimal sounds over slowed down house style beats. Some songs feature samples but synthetic sounds are more common. Works well at lounges and bars. Popular in Europe.

Prominent Artists Include
Bicep, Andreas Balicri, Sascha Kawa, Zuma Dionys, Mariel Ito, Timboletti, Serken Eles, Valeron

Funk, Soul, Disco
118 - 126 bpm

Heavily influenced by or sampling 70's funk, disco and soul music. Played over house 4/4 kick drum driven beats. Popular in gay clubs and USA.

Prominent Artists Include
Purple House, Joey Negro, Disco Incorporated, Funk The Beat, Thedjlawyer, Dimitri from Paris

Funky, Groove, Jackin House
120 -126 bpm

Samples and draws influence from classic disco and house records with a more updated and current sound. Works well as a warm up in commercial clubs.

Prominent Artists Include
DOD, Block and Crown, Richard Grey, Scotty Boy, Antoine Clamaran, Lissat, Agua Sin Gas, Basement Jaxx,

Future House
124 - 128 bpm

Big melodies using lots of strong sounds combined with hard hitting kicks and big build ups. Popular at festivals and commercial clubs.

Prominent Artists Include
Don Diablo, Mesto, Martin Garrix, Justin Mylo, Malaa, Mr Belt and Wezol, Steffi de campo, Swanky Tunes

Garage / Bassline / Grime
128 - 134 bpm

4/4 beats with a lot of swing. Wobbly basslines, stabs and some dark atmospherics. Some songs are more uplifting and funky, drawing inspiration from older styles. Popular in The UK and underground clubs.

Prominent Artists Include
My nu leng, Le Duke, Volac, DustyCloud, Phlegmatic Dogs, Ac Slater, Dram, Amber Mark, DJ EZ,

Glitch Hop

90 - 110 bpm
Big beats, with samples or processed effects. Very similar to hip hop or slowed down trap and breaks. Works well with dancing shows or in some small hip hop clubs.

Prominent Artists Include
Alias, K Lab, Staunch, Thomas Vent, Fort Knox, Grid Division, Popular Alive.

Hard Dance
150 - 160 bpm

Hard hitting beats, primarily driven by a big distorted kick and bassline. Big synth melodies or off beat bass lines and samples combine with the kick. Popular at festivals.

Prominent Artists Include
Headhunterz, Coone, TNT, Showtek, Technoboy, Darren Styles, D-Block, Timmy Trumpet, Brennan Hart, Ran D.

Hardcore and Hard Techno
126 - 130 bpm

Minimal arrangements with hard hitting sounds and attenuated melodies. Very dark and hypnotic. Works well at warehouse parties and underground European clubs.

Prominent Artists Include
T78, Pomela, Goncalo, Helldriver, Alberto Ruiz, ABBYVSM, Angy Kore, Oliver emmer, deker.

Hardcore and Hard Techno

126 - 130 bpm

Minimal arrangements with hard hitting sounds and attenuated melodies. Very dark and hypnotic. Works well at warehouse parties and underground European clubs.

Prominent Artists Include
T78, Pomela, Goncalo, Helldriver, Alberto Ruiz, ABBYVSM, Angy Kore, Oliver emmer, deker.

Hip Hop and R and B
70 - 160 bpm

Beats, rhymes and life. Most songs based around a vocal, either singing or rapping. Complimented by tight beats and cool melodies or sampling. Popular in most mainstream clubs in Western countries.

Prominent Artists Include
Drake, Rihanna, Beyonce, Kanye West, Post Malone, The Weeknd, Travis Scott, Arrianna Grande, Nicki Minaj.

House
126 - 130 bpm

4/4 driven by a consistent kick. Typically arranged with intro, break down then sixty four bars of drop. Very formulaic and designed for DJ's. Uses vocals, strong melodies and basslines. Works well as a warm up at most clubs or day time parties.

Prominent Artists Include
David Guetta, Bob Sinclair, Oliver Heldens, Natema, Riva Starr, David Penn, Paul Woolford, Josh Butler, Dennis Cruz, Leon.

Indie Disco / Nu Disco
110 - 124 bpm

Modern synthetic sounds played in a way that is similar to seventies disco and funk. Big electronic beats and catchy synth patterns. Works well as a background music.

Prominent Artists Include
Younger rebinds, Throttle, Kungs, Purple Disco Machine, Red Axes, L'imperatrice, Showbiz, Yuksek

Leftfield Bass
75 - 150 bpm

An alternative take on more popular bass driven genres such as house, trap and hip hop. Using different patterns or more experimental sounds. Works well for listening at home or mixtapes.

Prominent Artists Include
G-Rex, Peekaboo Wakaan, Nocturnal Sunshine, OAKK, DNA, An-ten-nae, ENiGMA Dubz, G Jones, Liquid Stranger, Dean Biscuit

Melodic House and Techno
120 - 124 bpm

4/4 Designed for DJ music. Long and progressive arrangements with kick leading and luscious melodies and bass play in symphony. Popular in European style clubs.

Prominent Artists Include

Guy Gerber, Maceo Plex, Adam Port, OC & Verde, Kolsch, Hale Bopp, Sasha, La Fleur

Minimal / Deep Tech
122 - 127 bpm

4/4 driven by a consistent kick and designed for DJ mixing. Simple melodies, clean drums. Hypnotic rhythms and long progressive development. Popular in European style clubs.

Prominent Artists Include
Low Rich, Stephan Bazbaz, Arkady Antsyrev, Archie Hamilton, Benson Herbert, Luuk Van Dijk, James Dexter, Nick Curly

Progressive House
126 - 128 bpm

Features beautiful melodies and breakdowns that build up to euphoric drops. Drops are driven by a kick, bass and typically a nice synthetic lead. Works well at festivals and clubs.

Prominent Artists Include
Alesso, Calvin Harris, Armin Van Burren, Thomas Gold, Borgeous, KSHMR, Dannic, Dirty Vegas, Avicii, Swedish House Mafia

PsyTrance
138 - 144 bpm

Bass heavy music usually constructed in a staccato stuttering fashion formed around a 4/4 kick drum. Synthetic fx and rhythmic melodies play over the top. Arrangements are long and progressive. Works well at festivals and in some open format sets.

Prominent Artists Include
Armin Van Burren, Vini Vici, Timmy Trumpet, Sphera, Outsiders, Protonica, Ace Ventura, Captain Hook, Gaudium, Animato, Stryker,

Reggae / Dance Hall / Dub
80 - 160 bpm

Most songs feature a vocal as the focus, usually a singer or some samples. Offbeat snare and percussion make up the beats. Bass lines and licks of instruments gel together in the mix. Works well played in live environments.

Prominent Artists Include
Joseph Cotton, Shy FX, Kiko Bun, Kalibwoy, Finest Sno, Darr3n Afreaka, Era Istrefi, Walshy Fire, Kalibandulu, Blaiz Fayah, Richie Loop

Tech House
120 -126 bpm

4/4 driven by a consistent kick. Very formulaic and designed for DJ's. Usually features the kick and a driving bassline as the main features. Some samples and simple melodies come in and out. Popular in underground clubs.

Prominent Artists Include
Tim Baresko, Shiba San, Green Velvet, Chris Lake, Dom Dolla, Eskuche, Solardo Sola, Mason Maynard, Pornographic

Techno
126 - 128 bpm

Very industrial sound with a kick and minimal instruments. Typically a kick and bassline with some samples or simple melodies. Arrangements are long and hypnotic, building up and breaking down. Popular for warehouse parties and European clubs.

Prominent Artists Include
Carl Cox, Thomas Schumacher, Victor Ruiz, Adam Beyer, Bart Skils, UMEK, Kraftek, Radio Slave, SRVD, Patrick Mason, P.leone

Trance
134 - 138 bpm

Usually features a vocal or huge melody as the main focus. All about creating a very euphoric build up to a harmony of sound. Long and progressive arrangements. Works well at festivals and niche club nights.

Prominent Artists Include
Josie Giuseppe, John O'Callaghan, James Dymond , Factor B, Yotto, Armin van Buuren, Darren Porter, Paul Denton, Craig Connelly

Trap / Future Bass
140 - 150 bpm

Trap is all about hard hitting beats and bass with powerful 808 kick drums arranged to create a breathing in and out slamming and snappy arrangement complimented by big sounds and tight leads. Future bass is more musical with layered complex leads and lush musical arrangements.

Prominent Artists Include
Herobust, Chainsmokers, Flume, Illenium, Saymyname, DJ Snake, Nitti Gritti, Habstrakt, RL Grime, Diplo, Jack U, Aazar.

How To Organize And Manage Your Music

Rekordbox

Rekordbox is a software for organizing your music library in preparation for use with Pioneer CDJ's. Before you start importing your music files into it you must make sure your files are not all over the place because if you ever change computers Rekordbox isn't going to know where to find the files. What I suggest is to create folders for each month of the year and put your latest downloads in there and then import them into Rekordbox to organize.

When you import new music you can analyze the songs to get relevant information such as bpm and length. There are two analyze settings, normal and dynamic. Normal is for electronic music that has a really consistent beat and dynamic is for music that may have fluctuations in the BPM such as live music or mash ups with tempo changes. if you import music that you know has tempo changes be sure to analyze with the dynamic mode. Then there's two analisis modes, normal and performance. The default is set to normal and basically what normal mode will do is not use too much CPU power when importing and analyzing tracks. If your DJing with Rekordbox on in the background, use this mode so that your computer won't eat up too much brain power. However if you want analysis to complete as quickly as possible it's worth setting it to the performance mode.

To import music you can drag and drop it into a new playlist. Rekordbox will then analyze the songs and then the waveform will appear. When you have imported music there might be duplicate entries. Rekordbox doesn't have a way to remove duplicate tracks inside a collection and the reason is because they're not actually duplicate entries they're referencing different music files. This is a symptom if your music is a absolute mess. Maybe it's because you've copied the same music file to a different location on your hard drive and you've imported both of them. Basically it ends up where you've got the same song or two copies of the file in different places on your computer. There's no way that Rekordbox can automatically determine that these files are actually called the same things. You can either delete the source file or go through your collection and click remove from collection.

Now that we've removed duplicates from our collection we're ready to create playlists. Playlists are logical groupings of music that allow you to better organize your collection and prepare for a gig. Clicking on the playlist tab will reveal a little plus to create a new playlist and it will ask you to name it. You can call playlists whatever you want as long as it makes sense to you. What I normally do is name them by genre. You can also create folders for multiple playlists. This is a good idea if you are playing lot's of different types of gigs. You could have one set in a folder with playlists and then another and so on. To add music to these playlists all you need to do is basically collect the tracks you want to add to the playlist, then drag and drop them into the playlist. You can also add tags to songs for labeling them in different genres or moods or energy, whatever you want. When you use the track filter setting on the CDJ clicking it will display this amazing menu where you can select to display by the tabs you have set up.

When your ready to export this music to a USB key or SD card for use in Pioneer DJ gear, simply insert the USB into your computer. You can see that it appears under the devices window within Rekordbox. Click Sync manager at the bottom of the screen which will bring up a display of three panels, iTunes, Rekordbox and your device. Clicking on a collection will essentially select the tracks to put on a USB key and drag that over to it's window. Or click the box of the lists that you want to export to your USB then click the arrow across. Exporting can take a little while and of course that all depends on the quality of the USB. When it is done, make sure the Rekordbox database has been finalized and then click on the little USB eject icon. You can then insert that USB into a CDJ supporting Rekordbox and your collection of playlists, settings and folder will appear on the CDJ in exactly the same way.

Mixed In Key

The perfect mix, doesn't just come down to beat matching, it also comes down to song selection and usually choosing two songs that are either in the same key or in similar keys. When talking about the keys of songs things can quickly turn very technical and you can just go down a rabbit hole of technicalities. If you are a complete beginner all you need to know is that all music is written in certain keys. You get major keys and minor keys. There's a few other keys as well but you don't need to worry about them. There are certain keys that go really well together and certain keys that just completely clash with each other. If you want to get that perfect mix it's better to blend keys in that go well with each other. The most reliable technique will be mixing songs that are in the exact same key or a closely related one.

Mixed in Key is a very useful tool to analyze tracks for key, tempo and energy level of a song. Within the software you can then add cue points and all data will be written into the metadata of the file which is in turn displayed in Rekordbox, Serato or whatever DJ software you use. There is also a piano keyboard so you can check the key by playing the root note to decide whether you think it's got it right.

Mixed in Key organizes musical keys using the Camelot system. The Camelot wheel is a system used to mix your music harmonically without having to memorize all the keys. When you first look at the Camelot wheel you'll notice it looks almost exactly like the circle of fifths with twelve key steps around the circle and each of those keys being a fifth step from the last. The key positions on the Camelot wheel are rotated five steps counterclockwise. Each key in the Camelot wheel is assigned an alphanumeric code ranging from 1 to 12. On the outer circle of the wheel are major keys and the inner circle are the relative minor key. Major keys are always labeled with the number and the letter B and the minor keys are always labeled with a number and the letter A.

Think of the numbers on the Camelot wheel like the hours on a clock.

To create harmonically pleasing mixes you can move around the wheel one step up or down, clockwise or counterclockwise while staying within the same ring. Each number represents a step up or down from the previous number. If you go forward or backward one step or within the same number then you'll have a harmonically compatible mix. Just be sure to stick with the same letter which just means that you're staying in the same ring of the wheel. There are some cool things you can utilize with this, maybe you to give some energy to a mix. Simply, step up the number clockwise to move to the next key like moving from 3A to 4A. The shift creates a lift in energy because you will be mixing into a key that is a fifth higher than the current key. Alternatively you can lower the energy on the dance floor slightly by going down a step counterclockwise such as mixing from for 3A to 2A. However that depends on the song you're mixing. For instance if you're mixing high energy songs when you go down a step it can actually create a unique effect of taking your audience deeper into your mix which creates a cool contrast to help you stand out as a DJ.

Some argue that you might lose creativity relying on Mixed In Key because you might ignore songs that aren't in the same key range resulting in missed opportunities in your mix. The bottom line is that it is not a hard and fast rule. Once you understand the system and your ears get more sensitive to the key signatures in regards to what melds and what doesn't then you can get creative and experiment. You will have intuitively trained your ear to be able to identify whole sections of music that are compatible with each other from different songs and you won't end up with any dissonant surprises. If you do get any key clashes at least you'll know it and won't play those songs together ever again.

Serato

Serato is a DJ software that enables you to organize and playback music with CDJ's or a controller. It is a pretty simple software as far as layout is concerned. It can be basically broken up into into two to three sections. First there is a deck section where the actual DJing happens. There are three modes offered for the decks. You have absolute mode which treats it more like a normal CD or vinyl. You have relative mode where you get access to things like cue points which you don't get in an absolute mode. Then you have your internal mode which actually bypasses the DVS part of Serato so instead of playing through the CDs or vinyl it's just playing straight through the computer and you don't have any physical control over it. There are upto four decks available, depending on how many decks you want to be playing. The deck overview shows you the song's bpm, time elapsed and the time remaining. To the right is the pitch percentage so when your mixing you can see how far plus or minus percentage you move the pitch. Each deck has upto six cue points available as well as loops from 1/32 to 16/1 timings.

Next is the library section and then to the right there is the playlists section. In addition there are other panels which you can open up to find files and there is also a prepare section below that. This is where you can hold songs that you might want to play next and you can simply drag songs in there. The history section allows you to actually look up what you played in the past. Maybe you had a couple songs that went really well together that you played the night before but you don't remember them off the top of your head. Serato saves all that information and puts them in order for you.

You can customize Serato into different layouts. The vertical layout which features the two decks side by side. The horizontal layout which puts the two decks on top of each other. Then finally, the extended layout which extends out the wave form even further and keeps a horizontal view. For beginners I would recommend the vertical view because it makes the most sense visually on the software. When you look down at your controller or your turntables or your CDJs it makes sense because it kind of mirrors where you have the song.

Traktor

Traktor is a DJ software that can be used to interface between a computer and a controller or a DJ mixer with two CDJs set up. Some controllers are made exclusively for use with Traktor.

When it comes to loading music into the software there are number ways to do it. You can load music from the computer hard drive or from an external source. If you want to use an external source ensure that is connected to your computer before you start Traktor otherwise it might not read it properly. Lastly you can add your iTunes playlists into it. Whatever you decide to use simply drag the music files from there location or right click import to collection and then place them in the relevant playlist or folder inside of Traktor. Like other music management software it is wise to keep files well organized on your computer.

Traktor automatically analyzes imported songs and can work out their length and BPM. You can analyze songs automatically one by one or if you're doing a batch, you can right-click on the playlist folder or track collection and select analyze. Make sure you don't do this when your about to perform as this will be an issue. If you have lots of tracks you need to analyze then make sure you run them when you have time to leave the computer, for example overnight.

After analysis Traktor will create a waveform and if you have the auto gain feature on it will set it so that you have similar amplitudes of songs. Finally it will set the song to a beat grid allowing you to mix in time. If necessary you can adjust this to get the timing of the track correct. If you want to use a sync function on your mixes then locking your songs to the grid is essential.

The track collection is basically your music library with all the songs, playlist and folders that you set up. There is an information window for your songs. The first column shows symbols and letters to give you information about the current song. For example a tick means you've already played it and an exclamation mark indicates that Traktor cannot find it. If this happens you can right click and relocate it or delete it from the collection. You can organize the collection however you want. For example by, title, artist, BPM, time, key and genre

Cue points can easily be created in Traktor. Typically you would place them at important parts of the song such as the first beat or the breakdown. When you press the cue it will continue playing from that point and if the song is not playing then it won't start the song but it will jump to that cue point. You can also add loops into the song and there is also an option to set a fade in and out marker. When it hits the fade-out it will automatically start the next track.

How to Mix Like a Pro

Theory

Right so now you have your knowledge, equipment and your set is ready. Let's start mixing. Wait, before you start mixing you first have to know a little bit about music theory. Hey, don't get scared! It's not that hard, it's all about counting to four. The basics you need to know are about bars. A bar or measure is made up of a group of beats that you can count so that you know where you are in the song. Music is written on a series of horizontal lines called a staff. A vertical line drawn through the staff is called a bar line. The bar is the space between two bar lines where the beats are grouped together. Notes are symbols that define how long a sound lasts. There are different kinds of notes and they all relate to each other. Mathematically the longest sounding note is the whole note. It lasts for four beats and you can only have one whole note in a bar. A little fraction code at the beginning of the staff is called the time signature and that tells you how to count the beats. The majority of club music is in 4/4 time. This means that there are four beats in every bar. The top number in the fraction represents the number of beats to count in each bar, which is four beats. The bottom number indicates which type of note receives one beat/count and in this signature it's the quarter note. Think of it like a dollar bill with one dollar being the whole note and four, twenty five cent quarters representing the quarter notes. Since one bar is four beats we count it one, two, three, four.

Standard Mixing

The standard mix is whilst a song is playing out of the main speakers you would have another song cued in your headphones.

First you select your cue point which you would have already set in Rekordbox. Usually it's the very first kick of the song. Whenever you press the cue or hot cue button you will hear it. Check the loudness of both songs to ensure they are equally loud. You can also use the metering on the mixer to help.

Next, match the BPM to the song you are mixing into. Now it's all about waiting for the right point in time to drop in. Tap with your feet or count one, two, three, four until your song playing out comes to a new measure. Typically in dance music its after four measures. With the fader down of the song in your headphones press the cue to start it. Depending on how fast your response is you will either have started at exactly the right time or you will be slower or faster then the song playing. If one of them is faster or slower it will sound horrible. You have to adjust by ear to lock them into each other. If it ever happens that they are not in sync anymore you can just push the jog wheel a little in the right direction. Make sure you always count to four and make sure that the beats are on top of each other. If you ever had piano lessons you know exactly how to put them on top of eachother.

But matching those two songs is not everything. The mixer in the middle allows you to mix between both sources. The song playing out of the speakers on one channel and the song in your headphones on another channel. Once they are locked in you can start to bring the fader up and fade one in whilst fading the other out. That's the most basic transition fading in one song and fading out the other one while retaining the beat matching.

It can be really easy to fall into the trap of mixing in and out the same way every time. Now there's nothing wrong with this but you can start to make your set sound quite predictable. Following on are some cool more advanced, mixing techniques.

Bass Cut

The next technique would be to actually do the same just a little bit more refined. What I love to do is mix in a song with the bass frequencies cut. You can use the low eq knob for this. I just kill it and after a few bars turn the bass of the new song in and cut the bass of the other one. It's like your switching the basslines up. This sounds awesome on most dance music since it is bass driven. Sometimes I leave the gap and just turn it all on suddenly, so the people feel the bass kicking in again. You can just kill the bass for four bars kick it back in again and get the people really excited

Mixing With Sound Color FX

There's of course a lot more advanced stuff you can do. For example you can use the mixers sound color effects. First you select them and control them with the knobs on each channel. When they're in the middle position they're off and then you can either turn them down or up. Try using the filter to sweep a song out. Try the echo to scatter the beats out. Space is really cool to make the mix go distant and wide. Use the noise filter to add drama to build ups.

Mixing With Beat FX

The beat fx section is awesome for creating unique mixes or for smoothing out transitions. Some of my personal favorites are the flange, phaser, beat rolls and delay. Flange I often apply towards the end of a transition or to suddenly bring in a mix. I

35

set it to be a long slow flange and then sweep the wet/dry mix to around fifty percent or more. Make sure you cut the low frequencies or mix over a break that has less lower frequencies because flange can really exaggerate the low end. For a more audible and crazier version of this use the phaser. Delay is great if you are switching tempos or stop the music. You can make the stop less abrupt by scattering over a little bit of delay. Beat rolls are great to use as a build up on songs.

Filter In and Out

Using the filters is a great way to smoothly reveal a new song. To start, make sure the filter of the song playing out of the speakers is turned off/in the middle default. The song cued in your headphones should have the filter knob turned all the way up. This is for a high pass sweep. You can adjust how extreme the sweep is with the color fx master knob. Slowly sweep the cued song in whilst sweeping the main song out. It will create a really cool and smooth mix.

Vinyl Stop/Drop In

The CDJ's have a setting for how quickly or slowly the playback starts and stops. It is on the right hand side. If you set it slow then when you press play/pause you get these long stops where the music slows down. Try setting it about twenty five percent and when your ready hit the play/pause button. This would be at the end of one song and at the same time or a little later, you press play for the other CDJ. That one should be a more instant start. It's a really clean way to mix two different songs and works well if your changing BPM. Another more extreme way is to set the tempo fader to wide. Then turn off key lock so that the pitch will follow the adjustments. Normally at the end of the night or at the end of the last DJ's set I would slowly, slow down the music to let the audience be aware of the change coming. Add some delay over the top to make it sound more pleasing.

Backspin

At the end of your transitions you can quickly spin back the song your mixing out. It's like a fast rewind effect. Be careful though, the back spin can sound quite loud and abrupt if not done properly so make sure the level is right and the low frequencies are cut.

Loop

On Pioneer CDJ's you can easily activate a four beat loop with one button. I like to add this on a longer transition. You could loop some phrase or melody whilst mixing the other song in. Then press the loop button again and again to speed up the loop and turn it into a roll. This is great for creating your own build ups and making mixes more exciting.

Mashing Things Up

Mashups will help you stand out as a unique DJ. Essentially they are combining different parts of songs that you like into one composite song. You might be thinking that's a remix. But they're different from a remix because the remix is when you take one song and put a different feel to that same song. A mashup is when you actually take two or more completely different songs and you put them together.

There are a few different ways to choose songs for a mash up. You can pick a theme such as, folk music, or pop music. Sometimes people like to pick artists and choose two different songs by the same artist. Sometimes people choose an older artist and a newer artist to show that the two artists are very similar. For instance you might pair a Bruno Mars song with a Michael Jackson song just to showcase how their songwriting styles are so similar. The best way is to listen to one song and then try to sing another song at the same time. If you can do that then that has the makings for a great mashup. Mixed In Key is great for this because you can easily identify songs that will work well together based on their key. Usually you would mash up songs in the same key or the next harmonic key. It's also important to have the same bpm but if its not then you can speed it up or slow it down in your editing software.

Mashups for DJ's often feature a vocal only (acapella) from another song on the break down of a different song. You could for example take a classic breakdown and mash it up with a newer drop. In other more advanced cases you can blend bpms. Say for example you are going from 128 bpm big room to 150 bpm trap. You could get two songs in the same key, edit where you want them to blend and then apply a tempo stretch in your editing software. This will help a lot when playing out live since you can effortlessly go from one genre to the next.

In addition to mash ups you should check over all of your songs before you play them out. Sometimes they might have parts you don't like that are too long or maybe need a better build up to keep the dancefloor energy. Edit these in or out using any digital audio workstation and then export to your music management software of choice.

How to Get Gigs

Before you start looking for gigs you need to make sure your skills are as tight as can be and that your library is lit. Get feedback on them, record mixes and ensure all is good to go. When you are ready to start hustling, start letting everyone know that you're a DJ. Not just on Instagram. Let any people you come across know that your DJ. I get calls all the time asking for me to DJ at a party. Sometimes they don't even know how good I am, but they just know that I'm a DJ. If you don't feel like going up to people and talking to them personally, you can hit them up on Instagram Twitter, Facebook, or whatever. It's all about getting the word out.

The next thing you should do is to check out if your area has online pages or profiles that promote parties. Search Google, Facebook and Instagram for your city + parties. Visit them and direct message them asking if they need a DJ. At the start you're probably going to DJ for free a lot which is alright because you'll be getting a lot of experience.

Another thing you can do is become a part of your DJ community. This involves meeting other DJ's and regularly hanging out with them. It can open up a lot of doors for you. I have met some DJ's hanging out a club and then of course our mutual interests form a bond. It's given me so much value, from being able to play at massive festivals to the hottest clubs. You definitely want to be a part of the DJ community. Find a mentor or a local DJ that you see gigging every weekend. Try to hang out with them as much as possible. Go see their shows, attend their workshops, whatever you can do to be around them. If you have a few remixes, mashups or your own songs share them.

They might think this dude really has some good music and they'll help put you on one day. You can even tell that same local DJ that if you ever need a DJ to come open up for you then you will be available. Or if you are ever running late and you want me to connect the equipment, let me know I can come do that for you for free. If you do a good job and the promoter and the club owners notice it they're going to say let's bring this DJ back again.

Make connections with companies that host events. Before you hit up these event companies you want to make sure that you're active on social media. Post content so it shows that you're legit DJ and not one who is going to show up and suck. An easy way to make content is to bring a friend to the parties with you and have them take pictures and videos of you. Once you've been getting more gigs and building up your social profile you can start reaching out to event groups and clubs. Search places on Instagram and look up a venue that you know hosts events or parties. Look for fliers, pictures or videos posted by DJs and then here you'll find like an event company logo at the top. You can then go to their page and direct message them saying something like, I want to DJ for you guys what can I do to make this happen? Build relationships with them, find out what they are looking for and understand their needs. When you message these event companies make sure to tell them that you have friends that will come because they love when you bring people to their events.

Go to clubs where the music is played that you love. Write down the top five clubs, bars and lounges that you want to go DJ at. Visit them and ask to speak with the owner or manager. Introduce yourself as a DJ who is interested to perform there.

Most times you will get a positive reaction since they are hit up on social media and online so much that meeting people face to face shows value and initiative. If you have a mix ready that really fits the style of the club pass it to them. In fact make a bunch of mixes. Do not aim the mixtape to the peak time of the club as it is more likely that you will play at the beginning or the end. Also don't expect to get paid so don't ask for payment. As previously mentioned at the start this is very unlikely. Be happy that you're able to play in front of people, if you are lucky you will get a couple of guestlist places and maybe some free drinks. But be warned, don't overdo it with the free drinks as this can go horribly wrong.

Management

At some point when the demands meet it, you might need management. They should support you, have a strategy for you, develop you as an artist and help you to jumpstart your career. This can involve, checking emails, getting in contact with labels, taking care that you get paid and all these kind of things. In addition a good manager should have contacts that help you.

If you have choices, do not pick the first one. Wait until you have like four or five people that want to work with you. Meet them and try to find out what their plans are. If they have a good strategy for you, believe in you, and you feel happy with them then it could be the start of a winning relationship. If you get lucky, your manager will be really ambitious and take consistent, massive action that brings results. Ideally you want someone that is already working within the industry and can help you to get connected with other people and pitch you to labels and all these kind of things. Before you sign remember that the management is offering a service and will be getting a percentage from whatever you are making. The standard is that the management gets from fifteen to twenty five percent. Everything above twenty five percent is just a ripoff. Don't even think about it.

Booking Agents

A booking agent is basically just like a travel agent. They will be taking care of your show dates, flights, accomodation and the negotiation for the money. The second you're so famous that people start writing you and want to book you is when you will need a booking agent.

How to get in contact with them? You can search directories or ask touring DJ's. Try and get in touch with them or make yourself so big that they want to get in touch with you. The best way is to make good music and regularly release it on the best labels.

When you work with booking agents they will often add their fees on the top. But be sure not to sell yourself short and also secure payment details upfront. Often you should be eligible for a fifty percent deposit before shows.

The fundamental key to getting bookings is relationship management. You need to be really good with people. Don't try to sell yourself too much and don't think your the best DJ. Understand what they are looking for and what they are not looking for. Get them talking about themselves and soon enough they will be curious about you and what you can offer.

Branding & Marketing

When it comes to marketing, content is king. It goes without saying but make sure that your mixing is on point because if the product sucks nobody is going to give a damn about you. Create a brand around yourself. Now when I say brand I don't mean you have to come up with some weird, wacky or wonderful DJ alias. Of course you should have a name that is cool and people remember it. But when I talk about branding I don't just mean the name you give yourself, it's about the whole package. It's about how you are perceived as a DJ and what kind of DJ you are. There are millions of DJ's out there. There are strict turntablists, resident DJ's who play regularly in clubs on a weekly basis, celebrity DJ's, mashup DJ's, producer DJ's and the list goes on. If a promoter puts you on a flyer it's not just about playing the best music anymore. You need popularity and good branding. Nowadays the popular DJ's have surpassed the talented DJ's.

How do you brand yourself as a DJ? It requires getting your name out there as much as possible. That doesn't mean spam. It's about putting yourself out there where a lot of people are going to hear about you. Connections are so important and you need to be constantly networking in the nightlife scene. It really requires being out seven nights a week. When you DJ put your brand out there, wear your logo, give out freebies with your logo on and have great visuals that show your branding. When people are taking pictures and your logo is in that picture, it is going to be circulated by the promoters of the party after the event. On top of that people are looking at the DJ booth when the party's going on. If they hear that you're playing well, then they want to see who is DJing and they will see your logo. Put it on everything, shirts, caps, booty shorts, you name it.

You can also create DJ drops that says your DJ name so when you're in party or mixing you can play them at anytime. Get your voice heard and get your name out there. Think of your brand as your flag, you're going to hold up that flag and wave it around for people to see that flag. It should showcase what you're about. If you can design your own logo and your own website it's only going to help you as a DJ. These extra skills will help you develop a style that you can then promote. A brand doesn't come to you straight away and maybe you need to experiment. Brainstorm and map out the different parts of DJing that you enjoy. Map out the different personality traits that you have, the different nights that you like to go to and start combining some of these ideas. Come up with something that says more about you than just I'm a DJ. When you're uploading mixes think about your brand, when you're uploading pictures to social media think about your brand. Think about how you can incorporate your brand into everything that you do. Grow that brand to the biggest it can possibly be. Try not to keep changing your DJ name, avoid creating new aliases hoping that a new name is going to suddenly give you some gigs because it's not just a name that gives you a gig. It's not just one thing that gets you a gig it's the whole package. Stick with it grow it as big as you can and then I guarantee you someone, somewhere will offer you an opportunity.

Producing

It's super important nowadays for DJs to produce their own music. You only have to take a look at all the touring DJs and Top 100 DJs to see that it's mostly producers. Producing music and spreading it to everybody you know and even don't know is the key for you to be a successful DJ. Make as many tracks as it takes for you to get to where you want to be. Post your music on all your social media accounts and make sure that the right people hear it and make sure that you grow a following in the process. A word of warning though, before you publically release anything you should send it out to record labels first. They will not sign anything if it has been put out for free download before. The first step you must take is to upload your music to www.soundcloud.com as a private link. Then you can share this with labels that have similar sounds. Just search through Beatport and then find the contact information through Google searches. Labels will often take a long time to reply so be patient and don't spam them with lots of low quality music. Produce the best tracks you can and try to expose them to as many people as possible. Eventually you will build up a fanbase and at the end that's all what it's coming down to if you want to earn and DJ more.

I can't stress to you how important growing a following is. The more followers, plays, likes, shares, and views grow your chances of getting booked. Gaining more requires being creative to stand out in a crowded market. Capitalize on what you're good at and if you're good at doing those things like mixing and scratching and doing tricks then capitalize on it. Get your phone camera or video camera and record yourself doing your routine. Record yourself doing your mix and post that up on all your social media channels. When you play out or even if you are just practicing, go live on Facebook, YouTube or Instagram at least once a week. If you see a club owner or a promoter liking your video, send them a message to say thank you so much for the support and start building the business relationship. Podcast your mixes you on the radio.

Produce more content featuring, slowly and surely your numbers will justify the reasons for clubs to book you. Sometimes you might put stuff out and it gets a low response. But don't get jaded, keep pushing. DJing is such a competitive thing to do nowadays and so setting yourself apart with your uniqueness and with your numbers is key to being a successful DJ. Practice hard, make that content and don't give up. Eventually if you make enough content that gets enough traction and enough numbers then you are going to be a successful DJ. Everybody who's successful in life is successful because they showed the world their tenacity, passion and drive to succeed.

Electronic Press Kit (EPK)

When party organizers or clubs contact you they will often ask for an electronic press kit (EPK) which is essentially a DJ resume. It is so important to have a very accurate and an up to date resume that covers the look of the DJ, the genre of music they play, autobiography and insight into the highlights of their career. When it comes to creating an EPK it's really crucial you work with a group of professionals. First impressions count and bookers are going to make a decision on the nonverbal communications. They will just go on the visuals and think I don't like that dude because he didn't invest in himself or herself.

The first thing to consider is a logo. Work with a graphic designer to produce a logo that represents you. Logo's are absolutely crucial, they should be memorable, well designed and represent you. Good examples include Deadmau5, Daft

Punk and Marshmello. You cannot mistake them for anybody else. Once you find something you like, stick with it and use it on all of your marketing material.

Next thing on your EPK would be the press images. Again work with a professional. Yes your friend might have a good camera. Or yes your friend might be able to take a few cool pictures with their iPhone but they won't have the technical ability to be able to do really advanced things. Professional photographers will help you stand out, utilize your best features and help choose the right locations. Their photos will usually be good for at least two years. I recommend shooting around twenty images in total. These need to be a combination of studio shot images, location shot images and profile images so that you have a real blend of looks to use. Also a combination of low key and high key images are great. For instance if you are a techno DJ the majority of your images would be more low key with a darker tone and darker clothes. If you are more of a commercial DJ then you want more colors for high key images. Your photographer should help you touch up and render your final images. Also your EPK should include the best images from your shows. Often clubs have an in house photographer so you can get those for free. If your just starting out ask a photographer to come and shoot your gig. Make sure you get one that has experience shooting in low light.

The next thing on your EPK is the biography. This would normally include, what made you want to be a DJ, what you are influenced by, what are the highlights of your career, what do you plan to do and so on. Social media links should also be included. All of the above would be created together in a PDF document that can be attached with an email. At least five to ten pages is the standard.

For example, you would have profile photo at the start with logo, then biography, some images of your shows, flyers and then social media links at the end. In addition keep a version of this on your own website. Make sure you buy a domain and hosting so that you come across as professional and legitimate as possible. If you have any videos of your shows that's great too because bookers can check out how you play.

For more ideas check out my website:

www.swindali.com

Everything You Need to Know Before You Play Your First Gig

Here are five quick tips you can use when you're doing your very first club gig.

Tip One

Be early. Don't be on time, be early. You definitely want to be professional and if it's your very first time spinning at a club, then you need that time to prepare. Especially if you are using some type of different equipment than what they're using. If you're plugging in your own stuff you definitely need that extra time to troubleshoot any problems that you might have. You will be able to handle the situation professionally, quickly and keep the night going.

Tip Two

Be professional, remember it's a business at the end of the day. You might be thinking that you're being paid to party. But at the end of the day you're offering a service and if you want to get paid and continue to get booked then be professional. Avoid getting drunk or chasing girls. Maintain a cool and friendly professional attitude at all times.

Tip Three

Lock down how you're going to get paid. if you can get a contract with the promoter or the business owner who's going to be paying you then get it in writing. Try to get a deposit which will cover you against cancellations. However in most situations you're not going to be able to do that. Sadly to say there's a lot of slack promoters out there and a lot of bad business owners who just really don't think paying a DJ is important. Be prepared for whatever may come your way. You might be put in a situation where you don't get paid. I mean definitely try to lock down how you're going to get paid and who's going to pay you and all that because it's really nice to get paid for your talent. But in the world we live in where everybody is a DJ don't be surprised if you don't get paid and don't let it affect your momentum moving forward because it often happens.

Tip Four

Make sure you have reliable equipment. If you're bringing in your own equipment to certain venues make sure it's reliable. The last thing you want is problems and the last thing you want is to cause problems for promoters or business owners. It might affect your pay and also might affect you coming back in the future. So definitely make sure that whatever you have and whatever you're going to be using is reliable, especially if it's your first time out. There are no excuses.

Tip Five

Last but not least don't be too cocky. This is really easy and can happen to a lot of DJ's especially when they're starting off and they build some momentum. The last thing you want to do is be that super cocky DJ because whoever's booking you and whoever you're going to be dealing with inside of those nightclubs and bars see many DJ's come and they've seen many DJ's go. You definitely want to be grateful for the opportunity to express your talent. Nowadays there's a huge problem where a lot of guys expect to play for hundreds but they've never played for a dead bar or a dead venue. Always be humble, when you fall from grace which often happens then those people below you will either push you down or help you back up.

How to Read a Crowd

Before you play out at any venue you need to understand what kind of crowd is going to be there and what taste of music they're into. Is it a young crowd? Is it an old crowd? Is it a ravy crowd? Is it a VIP crowd? There's all sorts of different crowds where you need to cater to but even playing from country to country it can be different. For instance trap is big in USA but not so much in the UK. In Brazil they like anything that has to do with Samba or like tribal drum orientated. You can start out with research, look up the venue and who has played there. Ask the owners and staff. Prepare your set in accordance. If you don't have the luxury of that then here are some tools you can use when you are mixing.

First of all arrive early and take a walk around the venue. Check out what kind of customers are there. Young, old, female, European, etc. Listen to what the DJ before you plays and observe how the crowd reacts. Feel the energy and the vibe, is the crowd really engaged or are they on their phones or are they walking on and off the dancefloor? It's important to take a mental note of this before you jump on because you need to really understand if you need to take up your set a level or perhaps bring it down. If you are headlining and have the chance to talk with the warm up DJ then let them know what kind of style you will be playing. Of course you don't want to play the same songs. If your the warm up DJ then be aware of the songs or genres to avoid and don't play too hard. Save that for the main act. You might be the first DJ on and no one's dancing. But if they look like they're having a good time the odds are that they're just really enjoying your set but aren't ready to dance yet.

When you are playing you want to keep the center of the dance floor packed and moving. If you have an empty dance floor then the crowd is not engaging anymore and you need to switch it up. Pay attention and watch the faces of the crowd so that you can still see if people are happy. Read their body language, watch for minor body movement like smiles, tapping at one's feet or nodding heads. You must also be engaged and be part of the party. Feel the music, don't be the guy that's separated from the party. Be together with the crowd, you make the party and if you feel like dancing then it's most likely the crowd will also feel like dancing.

When trying to read a room you can go all directions with it. You can give them more, you can give them less and if you give them less purposely then you can always come back with more. But at a certain point you'll lose your momentum and momentum is what it's all about. Creating the right moments, the right build ups and not just in one track but a storyline that you're trying to tell through your DJ set. Sometimes you could have a diverse crowd for example with pockets of high energy people, pockets of people liking hits, pockets of people liking underground stuff or new stuff or classics. Make sure your really flexible to keep catering to the crowd in any given situation. If you have a commercial crowd make sure you play something by DJ Snake or The Chainsmokers or whatever is hot now. If you have an underground crowd make sure to give them plenty of stuff they don't know. If you have a young crowd go for that festival vibe, play those EDM bangers, trap and dubstep. If you have an older crowd make sure you keep it housey and you can play plenty of throwbacks.

Reading a crowd is perhaps one of the hardest things to do as a DJ. If you can pull it off it will help you get more gigs in return. When you're in a nightclub you've got to be mindful of building energy in the night and not overstepping other DJ's. When people rock into a club the reality is that they just don't want to dance for the first hour or two. Normally they want to wait for someone to break the ice and make the first move. So if no one's dancing yet it's often a good idea to play to the women as they normally are the first ones to dance and then the boys will follow. The main aim is to keep the crowd happy no matter where you're playing. Being a club DJ you should be more about educating the crowd. Of course your often playing familiar songs to an extent but bringing your own representation of style and your music tastes to the table. Not just playing top ten hits, but really pushing the boundaries. However as a wedding or a function DJ you're just purely playing popular music because usually people there will only really recognize popular music.

Working with an MC

Some clubs often have a resident MC and their job is to hype up the crowd. It's great if you can have someone work with you who knows your style. I have worked with the same MC for years and you end up developing a great rapport. If it's someone new, make sure you have time to chat with them first. Share music and what your set ideas are so that you can gel and understand each other. You need to be in harmony with that person. If you are working alone then you might need to MC. But don't worry it doesn't require having an amazing, booming voice. Most crowds are drunk and all you need to do is

54

a hype them up a little bit. Put your hands up, are you ready, make some noise! These are all good go to, things to say. Before you speak into the microphone make sure you warm up your voice. You don't want to sound all hoarse and croaky. Use some basic vocal warm up exercises such as humming or ahhhs.

Dealing With Nerves

Your about to go on stage. Your hands are shaking, your throat is dry and your mind is blank. How the hell can you perform like this? Calm down. The first step to avoiding nerves is preparation. If you are well prepared and practiced then your confidence will be higher. There should be no holes in your set. Make sure you have a good idea of the place your playing and sound check if it's possible before. If you still feel nervous then realize that nerves are simply trapped energy. This might seem like a ridiculous thing to do but movement will release that tension. Jump, stretch, shout, pound your chest and get rid of that energy. Visualize your success and enjoy the moment. Remember that music is fun and you should smile, dance and enjoy it. This will be infectious to your audience. If you feel it, they feel it.

The key to all of this is confidence and you can always fake it until you make it. The one who believes in themselves the most leads and that is your job as a DJ, to lead.

Good luck!

FAQ and Top Tips

How do I deal with song requests?

Normally I would avoid requests unless they fit with your set. When someone asks your for a song, just say yes. Then they will go away and usually forget. Or say sorry I don't have it. If they are obnoxious, give security the nod.

How do I get the crowd pumped?

The obvious answer is to go commercial or mix in some classics. Usually people lose interest if the music is too new. You might also be playing too slow or too hard. Just think what is the opposite and try that route until you get more interaction.

What happens if my USB fails?

Always keep a back up. Whenever you export, do it twice to two USB drives.

How can I get more bookings?

Get out there and meet people. Add value, create content and share it. Increase your visibility by boosting your posts. Contact clubs and follow up.

How can I improve?

Practice makes perfect. Get a mentor and ask them for feedback. Record your mixes and listen back.

Where can I get mashups?

www.soundcloud.com www.hypeedit.com
DJ City
Or make your own.

What gear do I need to start?

A controller, laptop, software, speakers and headphones.

What if the warm up DJ is playing to hard?

Tell them manager or politely tell them yourself.

What if I trainwreck a mix?

Try to disguise it with effects and move on quickly. Practice makes perfect. If you have new music, test it at home first.

What if a club doesn't reply?

Follow up twice and then move on.

How do I score a hot chick?

Print business cards or have your friend go talk with them.

Should I drink?

I would not recommend it. But if customers insist then pretend to.

Am I too old or too young?

It depends where you play. Most clubs have an age limit of 18 or 20 and up. Your never too old, as long as you have energy. David Guetta is fifty plus and Carl Cox is almost sixty. Both icons.

Do I need to produce my own music?

You can easily get local gigs through hustling. Producing helps get you on a global stage. But if you are great at marketing or hustling then you can still get booked. Alternatively you can pay a ghost producer to make some hits for you.

About The Author

DJ Swindali has fast established himself as one of the hottest names on the touring circuit.

With new artists appearing every day, it takes nothing short of raw talent to stand out.

Born in England he drew on the country's rich heritage in dance music and began his rise to success sharing the stage with international DJs including, Chase and Status, Fatboy Slim, Goldie, High Contrast and more. In a natural evolution, he began producing music and was awarded a First Class Honors Degree in Music, was featured on BBC Radio 1 emerging talents and also set up his own record label to be distributed by Sony.

Inspired by the scene in Asia he relocated there five years ago. In this short space of time he has quickly made a name for himself, holding residencies at world famous nightclubs including his current residency at two of the top clubs in Bangkok, Route 66 and Insanity.

Major labels have taken notice of his music productions. Live Nation recently signed his collaboration with Ozmo on the hit song "Still Here", and "Overdose" with the famous singer Donyale Rene. Multiple times he has hit the Beatport Top 100 charts, has generated over 100,000 plays on SoundCloud and was rewarded three top ten's plus a number one mix on Mixcloud. All whilst growing a worldwide fanbase with over six thousand fans on Facebook, over fifteen thousand on Instagram and more counting.

Demand for DJ Swindali has seen him headline multiple music festivals, perform live on Fashion TV and conquer several famous venues, including Illuzion in Thailand, Sir Teen in Beijing, and several noteworthy appearances throughout the rest of the world. Including Shanghai, Malaysia, Taipei, Hong Kong, Cambodia, Oman, Myanmar, Japan, Vietnam and more to come.

Expect a high energy show tailored to your target audience, covering multiple genres, featuring originals, remixes, mashups and crowd hype to ensure a magnificent performance.

For more information

www.swindali.com

Thanks for Reading!

What did you think of, **In The Mix: Discover The Secrets to Becoming a Successful DJ**

I know you could have picked any number of books to read, but you picked this book and for that I am extremely grateful.

I hope that it added at value and quality to your everyday life. If so, it would be really nice if you could share this book with your friends and family by posting to Facebook and Twitter.

If you enjoyed this book and found some benefit in reading this, I'd like to hear from you and hope that you could take some time to post a review. Your feedback and support will help this author to greatly improve his writing craft for future projects and make this book even better.

I want you, the reader, to know that your review is very important and so, if you'd like to leave a review, all you have to do is click here and away you go. I wish you all the best in your future success!

Also check out my other books:

Music Production: Everything You Need To Know About Producing Music and Songwriting

Music Production: How to Produce Music, The Easy to Read Guide for Music Producers Introduction

Songwriting: Apply Proven Methods, Ideas and Exercises to Kickstart or Upgrade Your Songwriting

Thank you and good luck!

Tommy Swindali
2018